New Zealand

Land
of the
Long White Cloud

Graeme Matthews

New Zealand

*Land
of the
Long White Cloud*

Photographs
by
Graeme Matthews

Published by   Graeme Matthews Photoimage
                Blenheim
                New Zealand
                Phone/Fax 0064-3-570 5655
                E MAIL g.matthews@clear.net.nz
                Website: www.graemematthews.co.nz

Edited by Christine Cole Catley
Printed in Hong Kong, China
Photographs copyright © Graeme Matthews
This edition printed 2011

Paperback ISBN 978-0-473-03378-1
Hardback ISBN 978-0-473-02089-7

Photographs: *Cover:* Pelorus Sound, South Island.
               Half Title page: Maori canoe, Te Awatea Hou, Queen Charlotte
                   Sound, Marlborough.
               Title page: Southern Alps, South Island.

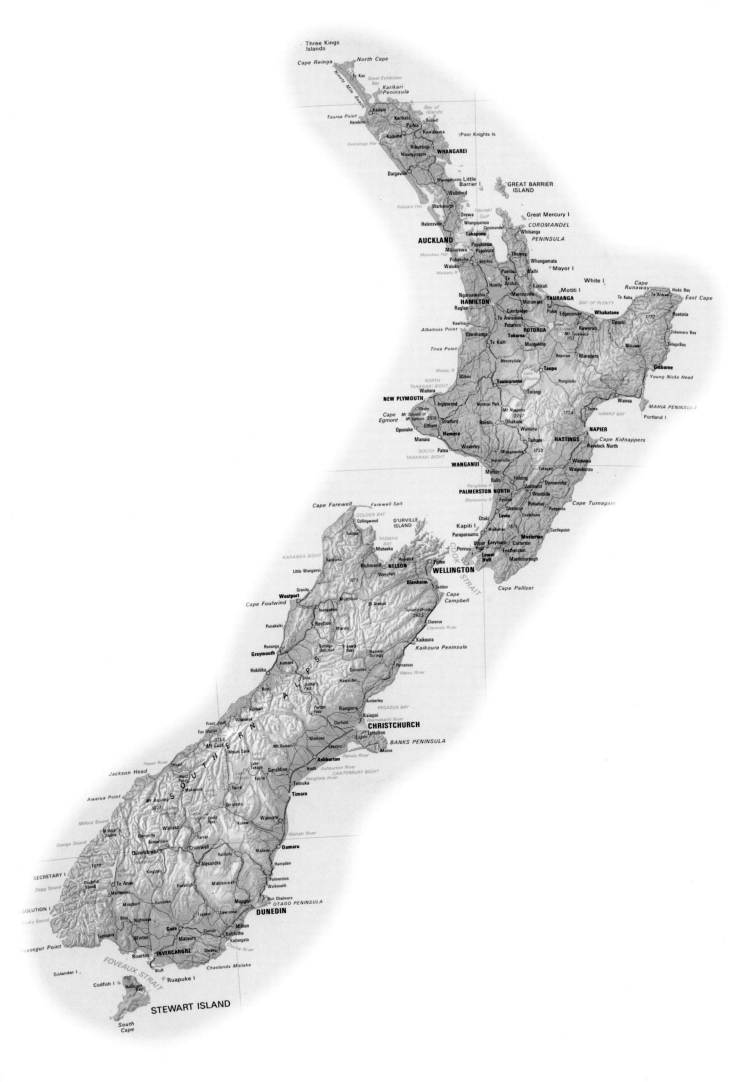

Introduction

I have called this book Land of the Long White Cloud because this was the very first name given to New Zealand. It is a name that seems to evoke the mystery and wonderful surprises that await the visitor to these shores.

The great Maori voyager Kupe named it thus when he first sighted land from his canoe, back in the 10th century. Then, as it often still is, it appeared as a long narrow band of white cloud along the rim of the ocean. One can only imagine the joy of discovery that he and his starving companions must have felt when they sighted land after so many months adrift on an immense and stormy ocean.

Time has brought change to this land which once enjoyed such idyllic isolation from the rest of the world. Maori civilisations have occupied it, living off its bounty of food, fish and birds.

The giant moa, that huge flightless bird more than four metres tall, roamed the countryside. Hunted by the Maori for its flesh and bones, it was eventually to become extinct. Sadly, this has also been the fate of many other special New Zealand birds. With the arrival of settlers from other countries, especially Britain, many species of animals and plants were introduced into a new land; a land which had previously evolved its own patterns of nature, without predators.

The cost of this colonisation has been high. Many birds have become extinct or are now very rare. Even the kiwi, that marvellous bird without flight that has become a symbol of New Zealand and its people, is difficult to find. The trees, too, that clothe the land have been challenged. Many of the magnificent native forests have been cleared and replaced with farmland.

But change has also brought about many of the features of New Zealand that are now part of its character. The countryside that was cleared of forest is green farmland now, dotted with 60 million sheep and 10 million cattle. The trees that the European settlers brought with them, to remind them of home, now add variety and colour to the countryside; willows, poplars, oaks and elms.

Even the cities and towns have their special character, brought about by the landscapes in which they are placed. The sheltered harbours, the valleys surrounded by hills, the plains, the lakeside and riverside settings where the towns perch — always these relate to the land.

It is the startling variety of landscapes to be found in such a compact country that helps make New Zealand unique.

As the two main islands straddle two different tectonic plates, (those great portions of the earth's crust that are moving and often in collision), the land has been twisted and distorted into the great variety of different landscapes that are now its trademark.

High rugged mountains, where the impact of the plates has forced the earth skyward, form the Southern Alps down the backbone of the South Island. The centre of the North Island has erupted in volcanoes and thermal geysers where these tectonic plates collide deep below the earth's surface.

When the land has been forced downward, the sea has rushed in to fill the valleys, leaving a mosaic of seaways that make up the Marlborough Sounds. The power of such steep glaciers on the South Island's west coast has carved out spectacular valleys and fiords.

Where else in the world can one do this — drive from the shoreline of an ocean in the morning, through rainforest, then farm pastures, between snow-capped mountains, across dry tussock grasslands, and arrive comfortably at the shoreline of a different ocean in the afternoon?

Surely a land to experience and enjoy, and to remember always.

Opposite: Coromandel Harbour, Hauraki Gulf

Above: Peacefully bathing with the seagulls: a young Maori girl in the warm, tidal waters of a Northland harbour.

Opposite: Along the full length of Ninety Mile Beach, surf from the Tasman Sea sweeps continuously in to shore.

Previous page: The Tasman Sea surges around the bottom of the cliffs on Cape Maria Van Diemen. In the distance is Cape Reinga, at the northern tip of New Zealand. From here, according to Maori mythology, the spirits of the dead leave the land to travel to the spiritual underworld.

Above: Nearly 150 islands make up the region known as the Bay of Islands. This has been an important area in New Zealand's history, for it was here in 1840 that the Treaty of Waitangi was signed between the British Government and Maori Chiefs.

Opposite: The Kauri tree (Agathis australis) is a giant of the New Zealand forest and one of the world's giant trees. Such was the demand for its fine timber that whole forests were cut down during pioneering days. Now only isolated majestic trees remain. The most famous is the tree shown here, Tane Mahuta, Maori for Lord of the Forest, in Waipoua Forest, Northland.

Above: Tess eagerly awaits landfall at Auckland city's waterfront. From here ferries cross to the opposite side of the harbour or to islands in the Hauraki Gulf.

Previous page: New Zealand's largest city, Auckland, is home to more than one-quarter of the country's total population. Its superb location around a large harbour, and with both east and west coasts close by, has created a special blend of city and nature.

The Auckland harbour bridge provides a vital link for a city that sits on both sides of Waitemata Harbour.

Above: A pattern of pohutukawa trees on East Cape, bathed in sea mist rolling in from the Bay of Plenty.

Opposite: The islands and rocky headlands of the Coromandel Peninsula; part of the wonderful boating region of the Hauraki Gulf.

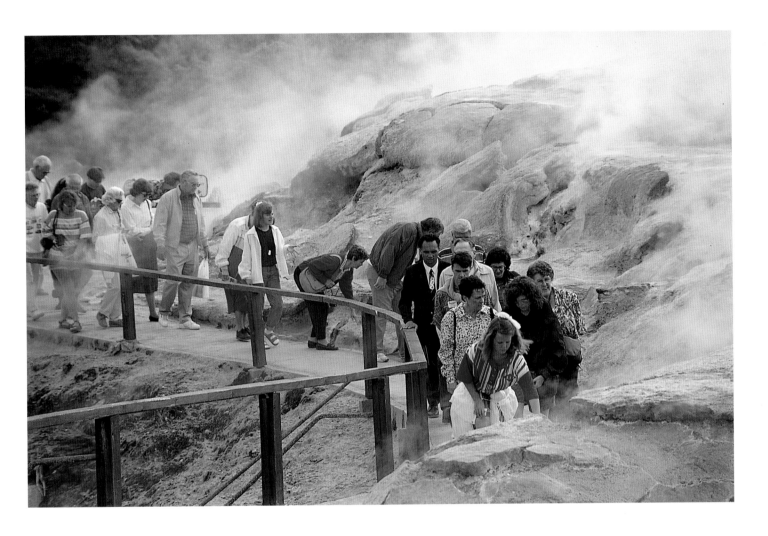

Above: An earth that is alive from within causes visitors to stop and touch its warmth; Whakarewarewa thermal area, Rotorua.

Opposite: The aggresive posture of the Maori haka. It was an important feature of Maori life and served as an outlet for every emotion; Whakarewarewa, Rotorua.

Previous page: The Waikato River twists its way through the lush farmland of the Waikato Basin. This is New Zealand's longest river, more than 350 kilometres. It begins on the slopes of the volcanoes of the central North Island, flows into Lake Taupo, (filling a volcanic crater), and makes its way to the sea through many lakes and dams.

Government Gardens, Rotorua, and the Elizabethan-style building known as Tudor Towers. It was once a bath-house in the days when Rotorua was built as a spa resort, world-famous for its warm mineral waters, geysers, hot pools and bubbling mud.

Watched by several hundred fascinated tourists, a sheep is separated from its heavy coat of wool; Agrodome farming display, Rotorua.

The Pohutu Geyser bursts into a clear blue Rotorua sky. Reaching 20 metres or more, it erupts at frequent intervals throughout the day; Whakarewarewa thermal area, Rotorua.

Making friends with the magnificent sheep which are stars of
the farming stage show at the Agrodome, Rotorua.

Above: State Highway No. 1 skirts the shores of Lake Taupo. Blue and peaceful now, it was once the scene of a violent volcanic eruption which formed the depression which now holds the lake.

Opposite: Seen from the air, Whakarewarewa thermal area presents a scene of chaos as seething cauldrons of steam erupt from the ground. The Pohutu Geyser is erupting and Rotorua can be seen beyond.

Above: Mt Ngauruhoe (2,291 metres) emits steam from its cone. This is the most active of the three volcanoes which form the Tongariro National Park.

Opposite: Near the very top of Mt Ruapehu (2,797 metres), the highest mountain in the North Island, sits a lake. This mountain is also a volcano and its crater has filled with hot sulphurous water to form the lake.

Above: The clear waters of the Tongariro River flow from the volcanoes of the central North Island into Lake Taupo, and have become famous for trout fishing.

Opposite: A good catch; a gleaming rainbow trout.

Above: Seen from across the sweeping coastline of Taranaki, the perfect volcanic shape of Mt Taranaki (2,518 metres), dominates the landscape.

Opposite: On the other side of the North Island is Cape Kidnappers, in Hawke's Bay. Thousands of ocean-living gannets come ashore here to nest and breed. According to Maori legend, the island rock in the photo represents the fish-hook of Maui, with which he caught the lengendary fish which became the North Island.

Above: Kumutoto Bay, Queen Charlotte Sound. This is one of the many sheltered bays in the Marlborough Sounds which make it such a paradise for boating.

Opposite: The Interisland ferry, Arahura, threads its way through Queen Charlotte Sound at the north of the South Island. This provides the link for travellers between the North and South Islands.

Previous page: Wellington, New Zealand's capital city and the seat of Government is known as "the harbour city". It is built on hills around a beautiful harbour, giving the city its special character.

Above: Covering the shoreline like a forest, seaweed swirls and sways; Kaikoura coast, Marlborough.

Opposite: State Highway No. 1, the main north-south route through both islands, hugs the narrow shoreline between the mountains and the sea; Kaikoura coast, Marlborough.

Previous page: Pelorus Sound, one of the main waterways that make up the drowned valleys of the Marlborough Sounds.

Above: The rising sun strikes the high peaks of the Kaikoura mountains while just offshore a mighty sperm whale spouts. Tourists on the Whale Watch boat gaze in awe at this spectacle of nature.

Opposite: Kaikoura Peninsula extends its jagged cliffs into the blue Pacific ocean. In the distance can be seen Kaikoura township hugging the shoreline, and beyond that, the snow-capped Kaikoura mountains.

Above: The west coast facing the Tasman Sea presents a rugged and wild aspect; seen from the coastal highway between Westport and Greymouth.

Opposite: Stacked layer on layer, the Pancake Rocks at Punakaiki are an enigma of nature. The action of the sea has eroded away alternate softer layers of limestone to leave a weird pattern in the rocks.

Previous page: Sunrise over Golden Bay, seen from Abel Tasman National Park in Nelson.

Punting on the tranquil Avon River – scenes like this have earned
Christchurch its reputation as New Zealand's most English city.
But the river's name does not have a Shakespearean connection;
it is borrowed from a brook in Lanarkshire, Scotland.

Hagley Park has been at the heart of Christchurch since the 1850s and is today its most significant city park. It is renowned for its extensive area of 165 hectares, its wide open spaces and mature woodlands.

Above: Bringing back the good old days; Christchurch has recreated a tram-ride experience, right through the heart of the city.

Opposite: Rail tracks that cross the width of the South Island. Seen here crossing the Waimakariri River, the Tranzalpine has become one of the great train journeys in the world. Beginning from Christchurch on the east coast, it crosses the farmlands of the Canterbury Plains, travels through the mountains of the Southern Alps, and descends through rainforests to Greymouth on the west coast.

Above: Sheepdogs eagerly await instructions from their master. Trained to find and gather sheep over rugged farming country, they are loyal and tireless workers for the farmer.

Opposite: Managing sheep on a high-country sheep farm.

Previous page: The Rakaia River weaves a tapestry of patterns as it flows down its wide bed of shingle eroded from the mountains of the Southern Alps.

Above: The Hermitage Hotel, Mt Cook. Set in a dazzling setting of alpine splendour, the luxury hotel has a long and famous history, dating back to the first hotel built nearby in 1887.

Opposite: Mt Cook (3,754 metres), New Zealand's highest mountain, dominates the view from the Hermitage. This beautiful peak was known to the Maori as Aorangi, The Cloud-Piercer.

Above: Towering peaks of rock, snow and ice form a backdrop to an aerial sightseeing trip.

Opposite: Flying above the Tasman Glacier, a sightseeing plane is dwarfed by the awesome mountain scenery.

Above: The special moment of landing by ski-plane and stepping out on to the crisp, sparkling snow of the Tasman Glacier; Mount Cook National Park.

Opposite: A kea, New Zealand's unique mountain parrot. Living high in the mountains, this inquisitive and comical bird endears itself to tourists — until it starts stripping the rubber from car windscreens.

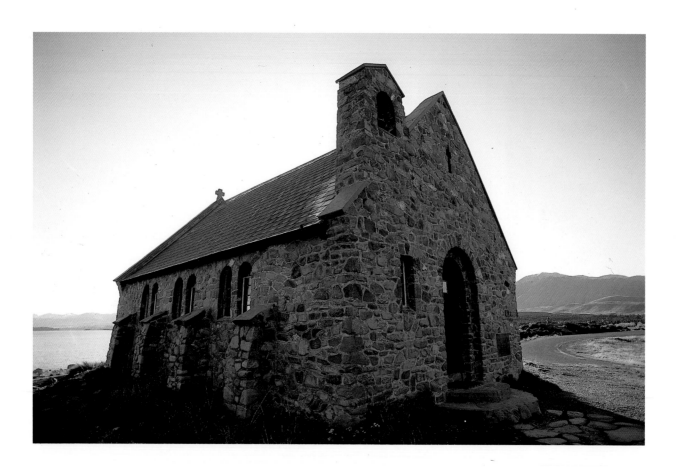

Above: The Church of the Good Shepherd, on the shores of Lake Tekapo. This tiny church was built on its beautiful location in memory of the pioneers of this region, known as the Mackenzie Country.

Opposite: Hot-air ballooning near Queenstown.

Previous page: Reflected sunlight on the many braided channels of the Tasman River, as it flows from the Tasman Glacier to Lake Pukaki. Mt Cook is the peak in the centre.

Above: Queenstown and Lake Wakatipu provide a stunning view when seen from the Gondola Lookout, 500 metres above the town.

Opposite: Throwing yourself off a bridge with a giant rubber band tied to your legs may not be everyone's idea of something to do on holiday. Bungy jumping, Kawarau Bridge, Queenstown.

Above: A street musician entertains a young family on holiday; Queenstown Mall.

Previous page: For more than 80 years the steamship TSS Earnslaw, known as The Lady of the Lake, has been sailing the waters of Lake Wakatipu. Towering over the lake is Cecil Peak.

With a full moon rising over the Remarkable Mountains, dusk
fades and the night lights come on in Queenstown.

Above: Between journeys the steamship TSS Earnslaw is cleaned down ready for its next voyage.

Opposite: Where miners once toiled for gold, tourists now come for a different kind of beauty; the rugged hillcountry of the Shotover River, near Queenstown.

Above: Arrowtown, near Queenstown, has survived from the goldrush days of the 1860s. Then it was a frontier town with a colourful history; it has kept enough of its old wooden buildings to give a feeling of "the days that were".

Opposite: Remains of an old stone hut, at Skippers, near Queenstown. The Shotover River was the scene of New Zealand's biggest gold rush, and for a time was called "the richest river in the world".

Previous page: The Shotover Jet bursts out of the Shotover River Canyon, near Queenstown; a thrilling experience these tourists will not forget.

West coast rainforests shield the high jagged peaks of the
Southern Alps; Cook River, Westland National Park.

Steam rises from the backs of cattle being driven along the scenic
Haast Highway to winter grazing.

Above: Tourists can be landed by helicopter on the frozen landscape of the Franz Josef Glacier and guided through the eerie world of pinnacles and ice-caves.

Opposite: Within a few kilometres of the ice-world of the glaciers one can be in the lush green world of temperate rainforest; near Lake Matheson, South Westland.

Previous page: The immense jumbled wall of snow and ice that makes up the Franz Josef Glacier dwarfs a tourist helicopter. The glacier drops steeply down from the highest mountains of the Southern Alps almost to the sea, making it one of the fastest flowing glaciers in the world.

Above: The Moeraki Boulders take on an unreal appearance in the early morning light; Moeraki, east coast, South Island.

Opposite: Dunedin sits snugly at the head of 24-kilometre long Otago Harbour. This southern city was first settled by Scottish settlers in 1846, and has retained many of the buildings and influences from these early times.

Above: Multi-coloured lupins cover the valley floor of the
Eglinton Valley, on the road from Te Anau to Milford Sound.

Opposite: The incredible road into Milford Sound. After passing
through the Homer Tunnel the road emerges into a world carved
and shaped by glaciers, and twists down the Cleddau Valley to
Milford.

Previous page: Lake Te Anau has several fiords. The South Fiord
shown here reaches into the mountains of Fiordland National
Park.

Above: Milford Sound. Carved out by glaciers and flooded by the sea, this hugely spectacular scene casts a spell on all who experience it.

Opposite: The Sutherland Falls, near the world-famous Milford Track. Plunging 580 metres from Lake Quill, the falls are one of the highlights seen from the 54-kilometre walking track.

Next page: The immensity of the sheer sides of Mitre Peak dominate the scene for a tourist boat cruising on Milford Sound.